YOU CAN BE A WOMAN™ BASKETBALL PLAYER

Tamecka Dixon and Judith Love Cohen

Cascade
Pass, Inc.

www.cascadepass.com

Editing: Janice J. Martin

Copyright © 1999 by Cascade Pass, Inc.
Published by Cascade Pass, Inc., 4223 Glencoe Avenue, Suite C-105,
Marina del Rey CA 90292-8801 USA
Printed in Hong Kong by South China Printing Co. (1988) Ltd.
First Edition 1999
You Can Be a Woman Basketball Player was written by Tamecka Dixon and Judith Love
Cohen, edited by Janice Martin. Book designed by David Katz and graphics by Grace Balnis.
This book is the first of a series that emphasizes the value of a sports career to self-esteem by
depicting real women whose careers provide inspirational role models.

Library of Congress Cataloging-in-Publication Data

Dixon, Tamecka, 1975-
    You can be a woman basketball player / Tamecka Dixon and Judith Love Cohen ;
editing, Janice J. Martin. -- 1st ed.
    p. cm.
SUMMARY: Discusses the life and basketball career of Tamecka Dixon, a player for the Los
Angeles Sparks in the WNBA, and describes what it is like to be a woman basketball player.
    ISBN 1-880599-40-6 (hbk.)
    ISBN 1-880599-38-4 (pbk.)
    1. Basketball for women -- Vocational guidance -- United States Juvenile literature. [1.
Dixon, Tamecka, 1975- 2. Basketball players. 3. Women Biography. 4. Afro-Americans
Biography. 5. Basketball for women.] I. Cohen, Judith Love, 1933- II. Martin, Janice J.
III. Title.
    GV886 .D59 1999
    796.323'082 -- dc21

                  99-20653
                  CIP

Dedication

This book is dedicated by author Tamecka Dixon to her mother Portia Dixon, who kept her grounded and helped her to never give up on her dreams and aspirations; to her father Russell Bowers, who provided the motivation and inspiration for her present career and future education; and to her coach Marian Washington, who provided the day-to-day motivation to grow, to take more responsibility and to be the best that she could be.

This book is also dedicated by author Judith Cohen to her daughter Rachel Siegel, who inspired her to work on this book by her daughter's love of the combination of skill, excitement, and grace that is women's basketball today.

The home crowd is chanting "Go! Go! Go Sparks." Suddenly an energetic female form appears out of nowhere. She moves so quickly and easily! Suddenly she breaks loose, drives to the basket, melting the defense, and then she spins into the lane and goes up for a right-hand hook shot! Tamecka Dixon does it again! The shooting guard comes in from the outside and sinks the two-pointer. And the visiting team is within two minutes of their first defeat.

Before the game is finally put away, Tamecka will sink a three-pointer from far outside and break up a play that the visitors were counting on!

This is all in a standard day's work for Tamecka. Today she scores 17 points while keeping the visiting team from breaking loose. Tomorrow she'll try to do it again.

How did Tamecka Dixon become All-American point guard Tamecka Dixon and later, shooting guard Tamecka Dixon, star of the Women's National Basketball Association (WNBA)? How did she find herself surrounded by teammates, racing to the goal? Let her tell us her story, the story of a new kind of athlete . . . .

I grew up in Westfield, New Jersey, in the northeast United States. I remember that I loved animals, and I loved school. I was always bringing home a stray dog or a wounded bird. And I liked all my subjects at school, but math was my favorite. But if you asked me to think about my childhood, I would probably think of myself out in the park playing ball: football, softball and basketball. I was good at these sports, so I was always the first girl picked for a team, and I hardly noticed that all my teammates were boys. It all seemed so natural.

My father, Russell Bowers, played basketball as I was growing up. He started taking me to the basketball court with him when I was three years old. As my dad was a standout player at American University in Washington D.C., I could think of a future for myself in basketball.

When my father was drafted into the National Basketball Association (NBA) for the Cleveland Caveliers, I got this idea that I would someday be the first woman in the NBA.

And when my dad suffered injuries that limited his career, he stressed to me that education was more important than basketball.

I listened, and after one bad year, I became an honor roll student at Linden High School while playing basketball for the Linden Lady Tigers.

Linden won two consecutive state titles during my years there, and I earned the "Most Valuable Player" title in both of those New Jersey state championship games. It was a very exciting time. I not only got to play, but I was also named a Kodak and a Nike All-American after my senior year at Linden.

9

My goal was to be recruited by at least one college that I thought would be good. Instead, I received recruitment letters from 300 colleges! It's hard to explain how special that made me feel. One of those letters was from the University of Kansas.

The University of Kansas was my first choice for one very important reason: Marian Washington, the coach of the Kansas basketball team, the Jayhawks. As soon as I met her, I felt that this woman would help me to become what I wanted to become, and that her guidance and support would mean a lot to me in future years.

Marian Washington was a great influence on the entire Jayhawk team. And we won. As we continued to win our games, she moved me from shooting guard to point guard. By doing this, she showed that she had a lot of confidence in me and required that I assume a lot of responsibility.

Remembering my early training, I was concerned about my education. I majored in child psychology and was named a Jayhawk scholar (and I intend to use that education later on).

I was also selected as a basketball All-American! Now, a few years earlier that would not have meant as much in the real world after college. But while I was at the University of Kansas, a wonderful thing was happening. The USA women's basketball team competed in the Olympic games, and there was suddenly talk of a women's professional basketball league.

In spite of my dreams, no woman has ever been recruited into the NBA, but now, when I was approaching graduation, I was recruited into the WNBA!

What on earth was the WNBA?

It's probably hard for you to believe that as recently as 1970, women's college basketball barely existed, and there were no professional basketball leagues for women. But in 1995 that began to change. The U.S. Olympic women's basketball team spent a year touring and working together before the summer games in 1996. And since they then won an Olympic gold medal in Atlanta, a tremendous amount of interest was generated.

Who were these women athletes? They were National Collegiate Athletic Association (NCAA) college players and All-Americans who, upon graduating, drifted into playing basketball for various European teams, or coaching for high school and college teams in the United States. Twelve of these women were selected for the 1996 Olympic team.

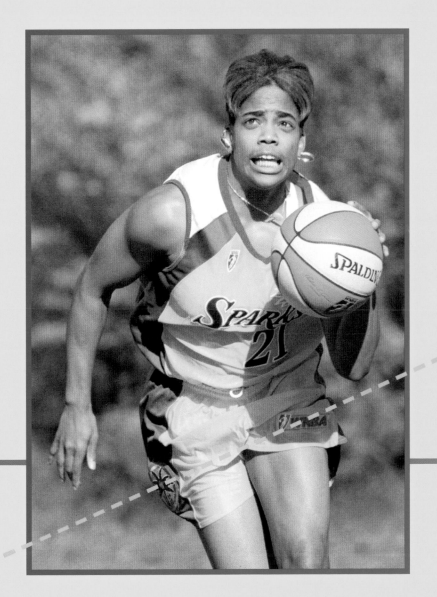

USA Basketball, the organization that created the women's national team program, had a more extensive agenda: to create a women's professional basketball league featuring the women who had starred in the 1996 Olympic team. In the spring of 1996, the Women's National Basketball Association, or WNBA, was founded. The NBA was a big supporter of this newly formed organization.

Eight teams began league play in 1997 with a ten-week summer season. They then expanded to 10 teams, and will soon have 12 teams, and an all-star game in 1999.

The Houston Comets, the New York Liberty, the Cleveland Rockers, the Charlotte Sting, the Phoenix Mercury, the Los Angeles Sparks, the Sacramento Monarchs, and the Utah Starzz of the first season were joined by Washington and Detroit teams the following season.

I love the game of basketball. There is very little left to luck; it is a game of skill. The objective of the game is for my team (five players on a team) to get more points than the opposing team within a set amount of time.

There are five positions to play: one center, two forwards and two guards.

Center: The center is the tallest player, big and strong but able to move quickly and score points. Ideally, the center is an excellent offensive and defensive player with terrific rebounding and defensive skills. The center is positioned closest to the basket for shots. The center goes for the jump ball to begin every game.

Power Forward: The power forward is a good rebounder who works closely with the center. The power forward plays within 15 feet of the basket.

19

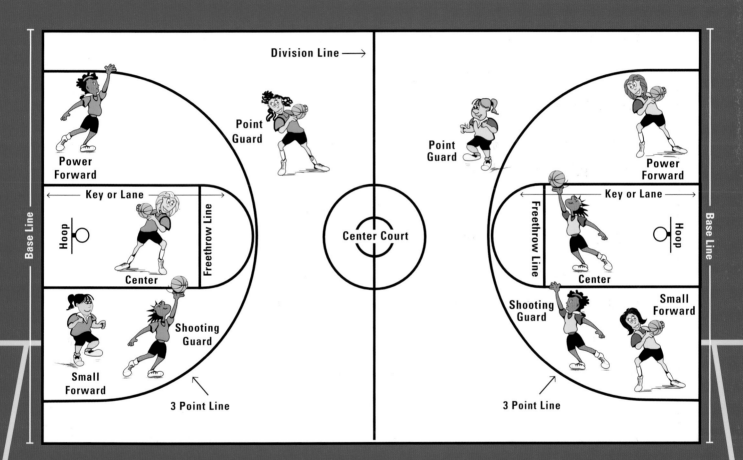

Small Forward: The small forward is positioned near the guards, shooting baskets from the outside or driving in the lane for the lay-up shot.

Shooting Guard: The shooting guard is an excellent shooter who has three-point scoring range (greater than 15 feet from the basket). Shooting guards need to be able to pass and work well with other players. I am a shooting guard for my WNBA team.

Point Guard: The point guard is the playmaker similar to a quarterback in football. The point guard often starts the fast break down the court and stays outside when the others fight for rebounds. I was a point guard throughout my college career.

Today, I am a member of the Los Angeles Sparks in the WNBA. The days in the season are full.

A professional needs to stay in condition which requires workouts. It's very important to practice often to make sure team members know the plays.

An example of a play: Once our team gets the ball, the two forwards run toward the lane. The other team's defending forward follows their moves to the lane. Now both offensive forwards are in the lane, creating an opening for a shot. The shooting guard, me in this case, moves to the opening and takes the shot, hitting the basket and scoring two points!

When the season is over, I have a number of special projects that are important to me. I love to put on basketball clinics where I get to meet young people. Today many of them are young girls who want to learn what is out there for them.

While the objective of the clinic is to teach a few skills such as ball handling and shooting, the most important message is for these young people to see that someone like them was able to learn to do this, and do this well, and that there may be a way for them to succeed also. They ask me many questions which I am happy to answer.

I often play ball in the off-season. This sometimes involves traveling to places I have only read about.

How can you tell if you would be good at basketball? If you can answer yes to the following questions, then you may want to try to play basketball.

1. *Are you patient and willing to work long hours to perfect skills?*

Basketball is a game of skill: free throws, jump shots, dribbling, etc., which all require practice in order to do them just right every time.

2. *Are you interested in working on your physical conditioning and stamina? Are you willing to sweat?*

In order to be able to run and jump for 40 minutes at a time, you need to be in peak condition. This requires many additional hours of running, jumping, dribbling, etc.

3. *Are you cooperative, willing, and able to work with others?*

Teamwork is the very heart of basketball. A single player doesn't get the ball down the field by herself, and the strategy involved uses passing and faking between players. My teammates are like sisters to me, and working with them is one of the joys of this game.

4. *Do you like to travel? Are you adaptable to new things and places?*

Basketball teams travel around the country and play away games as well as home games. And the reality is that today, many of us have to play in the off-season which may mean even more traveling. I enjoy the opportunities to travel, especially with my teammates.

What I like best about my career as a basketball player is the chance to use the skills that I developed during my childhood and growing-up years.

I've enjoyed the recognition I've received, first by colleges, then by the professional league, and now the Los Angeles Sparks team.

And I've enjoyed being able to do these things, not only by myself, but as part of a team, working together with these special women.

My future goals are to continue to play professional basketball.

I also want to return to school to complete my studies as a psychologist, eventually earning master's and doctorate degrees.

And finally, I would like to open a clinic to work with children who may need an extra push to achieve their goals.

I feel that many kids somehow fall between the cracks of society because they lack positive role models. So, with that in mind, I make sure that I am a model citizen for the kids to look at and gain inspiration from.

If you want to challenge yourself to learn physical skills and keep yourself in top physical condition; if you want to compete together with your teammates at the best professional level of your sport; and if you want to travel to parts of the country and parts of the world you never thought you'd see, then you can do it too. You can be a woman basketball player.

YOU CAN BE A WOMAN BASKETBALL PLAYER

BASKETBALL CLINIC ACTIVITY 1

PURPOSE: To learn ball handling.

MATERIALS: Basketball, space.

PROCEDURES: First have the girls practice holding the ball with both hands, not just the fingers. Have them feel its size and weight and move it around with their hands until it feels comfortable.

Have girls in pairs. Have each pair practice passing the ball back and forth, first facing one another and then side-by-side.

Have girls practice dribbling the ball in place, passing it from their right hands to their left hands. Finally, when comfortable, have them try dribbling while walking and then while running. Girls should move from side-to-side, bringing the ball to their left side and then to their right side.

CONCLUSIONS: Keeping control of the ball is very important. And remind them: "Remember you can't just keep your eye on the ball, since you need to keep you eyes on the other players; you need to be able to feel where the ball is."

BASKETBALL CLINIC ACTIVITY 2

PURPOSE: To learn proper "shooting" technique.

MATERIALS: Basketball hoop with backboard and basketball.

PROCEDURES: Have each girl practice the starting position: bent knees, hands on either side of the ball, ball out in front and above her head. The arm is bent in an L shape. Have the girls practice straightening knees and straightening arms together (without letting go of the ball) until they can do it rhythmically.

Finally, have each girl aim at the spot behind and above the basket, so that the ball will bounce into it from the backboard. Let each girl take four shots and see if she can score a basket.

CONCLUSIONS: Before they can shoot baskets while running, dribbling, and jumping, girls must learn how to hit a basket while standing still and aiming. A very good free-throw percentage is a must. It's like free points.

BASKETBALL CLINIC ACTIVITY 3

PURPOSE: To have a little fun playing the game "knockout" while practicing "shooting."

MATERIALS: Basketball hoop with backboard, basketball.

PROCEDURES: Have girls all line up. Let each one take one shot at the basket. If she misses she can go to the end of the line and continue to try, but if the girl behind her makes the shot before she does, than she is out of the game. If she makes it, she is still in and goes to the end of the line. The last girl left in at the end is the winner.

CONCLUSIONS: It takes practice to be able to reliably shoot a ball into a basket, even when you have time to aim and don't have to fight off the defense. Remind them to : "Practice!!!"

About the Authors:

Tamecka Dixon is now a member of the Los Angeles Sparks professional basketball team in the Women's National Basketball Association (WNBA). Prior to this, she attended the University of Kansas where she played spectacular basketball (All-American) while earning her bachelor's degree in child psychology. While Tamecka played the position of point guard at the University of Kansas, she has reinvented herself as a shooting guard for the L.A. Sparks. She plans to go back to school to complete her advanced degrees in psychology so that she can work with children in that capacity in the future.

Judith Love Cohen is a Registered Professional Electrical Engineer with bachelor's and master's degrees in engineering from the University of Southern California and University of California, Los Angeles. She has written plays, screenplays, and newspaper articles in addition to her series of children's books that began with *You Can Be a Woman Engineer*.

Acknowledgments:
Maxine Lachman for research and contributions on sports.
Photos by Rich Schultz: Pgs. 15, 23, 25, 27, 31, 33, 35, and cover.
Photos courtesy of NBA: Garrett Ellwood, Pgs. 17 & 21; Andrew D. Bernstein, Pg.5;
Bill Baptist, Pg. 29; Barry Gossage, Pg. 3; Rocky Widrer, Pg. 13.
Photo courtesy of University of Kansas: Pg. 11.
Photos courtesy of Tamecka Dixon: Pgs. 7 & 9